21 PSYCHOLOGICAL TRIGGERS

TO MAKE YOUR EX **BEG YOU** FOR A SECOND CHANCE

21 PSYCHOLOGICAL TRIGGERS TO MAKE YOUR EX BEG YOU FOR A SECOND CHANCE

INTRODUCTION

The Pain of Losing Her

There's no pain quite like the agony of losing the woman you love. One moment, your world is full of warmth, laughter, and shared dreams. The next, you're plunged into a cold, dark void where her absence consumes your every thought. The memories that once brought joy now twist like knives in your gut. Her smile, her touch, her scent – all haunt you mercilessly.

You find yourself struggling to eat, to sleep, to focus on anything but the gaping hole she's left in your life. The future you'd planned together crumbles before your eyes, leaving you lost and adrift. Every song on the radio seems to mock your pain. Every happy couple you see is a bitter reminder of what you've lost.

21 PSYCHOLOGICAL TRIGGERS TO MAKE YOUR EX BEG YOU FOR A SECOND CHANCE

INTRODUCTION

The worst part? The powerlessness. The feeling that no matter what you do, you can't change her mind. That she's slipping away, and there's nothing you can do to stop it. You'd give anything to turn back time, to fix whatever went wrong. But as the days pass and her silence grows, that hope feels increasingly desperate.

This guide understands your pain. It recognizes the depth of your loss and the intensity of your desire to win her back. But more importantly, it offers you a way out of this darkness — a proven path back to her heart.

Why Most Men Fail to Get Their Ex Back

If you've already tried to win her back, you've likely realized it's not as simple as grand gestures or heartfelt pleas. In fact, many of the instinctive actions men take after a breakup actually push their ex further away. Here's why most attempts fail:

- **Desperation and neediness:** When you're hurting, it's natural to want to reach out constantly, to beg and plead for another chance. But this behavior is deeply unattractive to women. It signals weakness and insecurity, often confirming her decision to leave.
- **Misunderstanding her emotions:** Men often misinterpret a woman's actions after a breakup, leading to further missteps. Her coldness might be a defense mechanism, not a sign she doesn't care. Her anger might mask hurt, not hatred.

INTRODUCTION

- **Trying to logic her back:** Many men attempt to "reason" their way back into a relationship, presenting logical arguments for why they should be together. But attraction and love aren't logical – they're deeply emotional.
- **Moving too fast:** In their eagerness to reconcile, men often push for too much, too soon. This overwhelms their ex and robs her of the space she needs to miss them.
- **Failing to address root issues:** Getting back together without resolving the underlying problems that led to the breakup is a recipe for repeated heartbreak.
- **Neglecting self-improvement:** Many men focus solely on winning her back, forgetting that becoming a better version of themselves is crucial to reigniting her attraction.
- **Playing manipulative games:** While some "pickup artist" tactics might seem tempting, they often backfire, damaging trust and genuine connection.
- **Giving up too soon:** On the flip side, some men throw in the towel at the first sign of resistance, not realizing that patience and persistence (applied correctly) are often key.

What This Guide Will Teach You
This isn't just another collection of cliché relationship advice. "21 Psychological Triggers to Make Her Beg You for a Second Chance" is a comprehensive, science-based system designed to tap into the deepest core of female psychology. Here's what you'll learn:

21 PSYCHOLOGICAL TRIGGERS TO MAKE YOUR EX BEG YOU FOR A SECOND CHANCE

INTRODUCTION

- **The hidden reasons behind your breakup:** We'll uncover the true causes she may not even be consciously aware of, giving you invaluable insight into her mind.
- **How to master the crucial "No Contact" period:** You'll learn exactly how long to maintain radio silence and what to do during this time to dramatically increase your chances of reconciliation.
- **Decoding her behavior:** Never be confused by her mixed signals again. You'll gain the ability to read her actions like an open book, understanding her true feelings and intentions.
- **Powerful re-attraction triggers:** Discover psychological techniques that bypass her logical mind and speak directly to her emotions, making her obsess over you again.
- **Dealing with competition:** Even if she's seeing someone new, you'll learn how to outshine any rival and reclaim your place in her heart.
- **Reigniting passion and desire:** Go beyond just getting her back – learn how to make her fall more deeply in love with you than ever before.
- **Long-term relationship success:** Ensure this is the last breakup you'll ever have to endure by mastering the art of keeping her hopelessly devoted to you.

This guide combines cutting-edge psychological research with real-world tested techniques. It's not about manipulation or games – it's about understanding the female mind on a profound level and using that knowledge to create a genuine, lasting connection.

21 PSYCHOLOGICAL TRIGGERS TO MAKE YOUR EX BEG YOU FOR A SECOND CHANCE

INTRODUCTION

By the time you finish this guide, you'll have a clear, step-by-step roadmap to winning her back. More than that, you'll have the tools to become the man she can't help but want – the man she'll fight to keep in her life.

Are you ready to transform your pain into the fuel that will drive you back into her arms? Let's begin.

PART 1:

Decoding Her True Feelings

21 Psychological Triggers to Make Her
Beg You for a Second Chance

PART 1: DECODING HER TRUE FEELINGS

Discover Why She Really Left

Understanding why your ex truly left is crucial for any hope of reconciliation. Often, the reasons she gives aren't the full story. Let's explore the hidden factors that likely drove her decision.

The 5 Hidden Reasons Women Leave
- **Loss of Attraction:** In over 90% of breakups, the core reason is a loss of sexual attraction. This isn't about physical appearance, but rather about behavioral patterns that diminish her desire for you.

21 PSYCHOLOGICAL TRIGGERS TO MAKE YOUR EX BEG YOU FOR A SECOND CHANCE

PART 1: DECODING HER TRUE FEELINGS

- Women are hardwired to be attracted to confident, self-assured men. If you've been displaying neediness, insecurity, or an inability to stand up for yourself, it erodes her attraction over time.
- **Lack of Emotional Connection:** Women crave deep emotional intimacy. If you've been emotionally unavailable, unable to communicate effectively, or haven't been "speaking her heart," she may feel disconnected even if everything else seems fine. Many men make the mistake of thinking providing financially or being physically present is enough.
- **Feeling Underappreciated:** Women want to feel cherished and valued in a relationship. If you've been taking her for granted, failing to acknowledge her contributions, or not making her feel special, resentment can build silently until she reaches a breaking point.
- **Lack of Progress:** If the relationship isn't "moving forward" in her eyes, she may leave out of frustration. This is especially common for women in their early to mid-thirties who feel their biological clock ticking. If you're not ready to take the next step (whatever that may be in your relationship), she might decide to find someone who is.
- **Unresolved Conflict or Constant Criticism:** Dr. John Gottman's research shows that contempt is the number one predictor of divorce. If your relationship has been filled with constant nagging, criticism, or unresolved arguments, it creates a toxic environment that pushes her away.

PART 1: DECODING HER TRUE FEELINGS

Uncovering the Truth She Won't Tell You
- **Look Beyond Her Words:** Women often give "softer" reasons for breaking up to spare your feelings. Phrases like "It's not you, it's me" or "We're better as friends" are usually cover-ups for deeper issues. Don't take these at face value.
- **Analyze Her Behavior:** Actions speak louder than words. Has she been distant? Less affectionate? Spending more time away from you? These can be clues to her true feelings.
- **Reflect on Recent Changes:** Did she suddenly start getting a lot of texts when you were together? Was she becoming more secretive with her phone? These could indicate she was already emotionally or physically connecting with someone else before the breakup.
- **Consider Timing:** If the breakup seemed to come out of nowhere, it's likely she's been considering it for a while. Women often spend weeks or months emotionally disconnecting before actually ending the relationship.
- **Examine Your Own Behavior:** Be honest with yourself. Have you been controlling? Jealous? A "pushover"? Constantly depressed or complaining? These behaviors are major attraction-killers and could be the real reason she left.
- **Understand the Chemical Factor:** Remember, love involves powerful brain chemicals. When a woman leaves, it's often because these "love chemicals" (like serotonin and vasopressin) have diminished. It's not always about you personally, but about the chemical cocktail in her brain.

PART 1: DECODING HER TRUE FEELINGS

By understanding these hidden reasons and learning to read between the lines, you can gain crucial insight into her true motivations. This knowledge is essential for addressing the real issues and rekindling her attraction and love for you.

In the next section, we'll explore how to navigate the emotional stages she's going through post-breakup, ensuring you don't make critical mistakes as you work towards reconciliation.

Her Secret Emotional Stages
Understanding her emotional journey post-breakup and gauging where she's at emotionally are crucial steps in your journey to win her back. Women go through a complex series of emotional stages after a breakup, and knowing where she is in this process can help you tailor your approach for maximum impact.

Understanding Her Emotional Journey Post-Breakup
Women typically go through five distinct stages after a breakup, similar to the stages of grief. Being aware of these stages will help you navigate the reconciliation process more effectively:

- **Denial and Isolation:** In this initial stage, she may act as if the breakup hasn't really happened. She might still reach out to you, maintain contact, or even suggest staying friends. This is her way of cushioning the emotional blow and avoiding the pain of the loss.

PART 1: DECODING HER TRUE FEELINGS

- **Anger:** As reality sets in, she may become angry or resentful. This anger could be directed at you, herself, or the situation in general. She might lash out, criticize you to friends, or suddenly become cold and distant.
- **Bargaining:** In this stage, she might start to wonder if the breakup was a mistake. She may reach out to "check on you" or suggest casual meetups. However, this doesn't necessarily mean she wants to get back together – it's often a way of testing the waters and easing her guilt.
- **Depression:** This is when the full weight of the loss hits her. She may withdraw from social activities, seem sad or listless, and spend a lot of time alone. This stage can last for varying lengths of time, depending on the individual and the relationship.
- **Acceptance:** Finally, she comes to terms with the breakup. She starts to move on with her life, possibly dating again or focusing on personal goals. Paradoxically, this is often the best time to reignite her interest, as she's emotionally stable enough to consider reconciliation without the baggage of earlier stages.

How to Gauge Where She's At Emotionally
Determining which stage your ex is in can be tricky, but there are several indicators you can look for:

- **Analyze Her Communication Patterns:**
    - Frequent, emotional contact suggests she's in the denial or bargaining stage.
    - Angry or accusatory messages indicate she's in the anger phase.

PART 1: DECODING HER TRUE FEELINGS

- Monitor Her Social Media Activity:
    - Increased posting or partying photos often signal the denial stage.
    - Melancholy or introspective posts could indicate depression.
    - A return to normal posting habits or positive life updates suggest acceptance.
- Pay Attention to Mutual Friends:
    - If she's asking about you frequently, she's likely in denial or bargaining.
    - Negative comments about you to friends usually indicate anger.
    - If friends report she seems down or withdrawn, she's probably in the depression stage.
- Notice Her Reaction to You:
    - If she seems overly emotional or tries to maintain close contact, she's in early stages.
    - Complete indifference or politeness might indicate she's moving towards acceptance.
- Observe Her Life Changes:
    - Drastic changes in appearance or lifestyle often occur in the depression or acceptance stages.
    - Throwing herself into work or hobbies could be a sign of moving towards acceptance.
- Consider the Time Frame: While everyone processes breakups differently, there's often a general timeline:
    - Denial and anger typically occur in the first few weeks.
    - Bargaining and depression can last for several months.

PART 1: DECODING HER TRUE FEELINGS

- Acceptance usually begins around 3-6 months post-breakup, depending on the relationship length.

Understanding these stages and accurately gauging her emotional state is crucial for several reasons:
- It helps you avoid pushing too hard when she's not ready.
- It allows you to time your re-attraction efforts for maximum impact.
- It gives you insight into her thought process, helping you address her emotional needs.
- It prevents you from misinterpreting her actions and making poor decisions based on false hope.

Remember, these stages aren't always linear. She may bounce back and forth between them or experience multiple stages simultaneously. Your job is to be patient, observant, and ready to adjust your strategy based on her emotional state.

In the next section, we'll explore how to use this understanding to craft messages and actions that resonate with her current emotional stage, increasing your chances of successful reconciliation.

Decoding Her Cryptic Messages and Social Media Posts
Understanding what your ex is really saying can be challenging, especially when she's not being direct. Women often communicate in subtle ways, leaving you to decipher their true intentions.

PART 1: DECODING HER TRUE FEELINGS

Let's break down how to read between the lines of her texts, interpret her social media behavior, and recognize body language cues that reveal her true feelings.

Reading Between the Lines of Her Texts
- **Frequency and Length:**
    - Frequent, lengthy messages suggest she's still emotionally invested.
    - Short, infrequent replies may indicate she's trying to create distance.
- **Response Time:**
    - Quick responses show you're a priority.
    - Delayed replies might mean she's deliberately trying to seem less available.
- **Content and Tone:**
    - Emotionally charged messages (positive or negative) indicate she still cares.
    - Neutral, formal tone could suggest she's trying to maintain boundaries.
- **Use of Emojis:**
    - Frequent use of emojis, especially hearts or flirty faces, suggests warmth and interest.
    - Lack of emojis in previously emoji-filled conversations may indicate emotional withdrawal.
- **Topics of Conversation:**
    - Bringing up shared memories or inside jokes shows she's reminiscing about your relationship.
    - Sticking to purely practical matters might mean she's trying to keep things impersonal.

PART 1: DECODING HER TRUE FEELINGS

- **Questions and Engagement:**
    - If she asks questions about your life, she's showing interest.
    - One-word answers or lack of questions could mean she's trying to discourage further communication.

Remember, context is key. A seemingly cold message could be due to her being busy or having a bad day, not necessarily a reflection of her feelings for you.

Interpreting Her Social Media Behavior

Social media can provide valuable insights into her state of mind and feelings towards you:

- **Post Frequency:**
    - Increased posting often indicates she's trying to show she's doing fine without you.
    - Decreased activity might mean she's withdrawing or feeling down.
- **Content of Posts:**
    - Upbeat, party-focused posts soon after a breakup often mask pain (denial stage).
    - Melancholy quotes or song lyrics could be indirect messages about her feelings.
    - Posts about self-improvement or new hobbies might indicate she's moving towards acceptance.
- **Interaction with Your Posts:**
    - Likes or comments on your posts suggest she's still interested in your life.
    - Complete avoidance of your social media presence could mean she's trying to move on.

21 PSYCHOLOGICAL TRIGGERS TO MAKE YOUR EX BEG YOU FOR A SECOND CHANCE

PART 1: DECODING HER TRUE FEELINGS

- **Mutual Friends:**
    - If she's still interacting with your friends online, she might be trying to maintain a connection to your world.
- **Relationship Status:**
    - Keeping her status as "In a Relationship" or not updating it could mean she's not ready to publicly acknowledge the breakup.
- **Photos and Check-ins:**
    - Posting lots of group photos might be a way to show she has support and is socializing.
    - Check-ins at places you used to frequent together could be a subtle message to you.
- **Stories and Temporary Posts:**
    - Pay attention to fleeting content like Instagram stories. She might post things here she wouldn't on her main feed, offering more authentic glimpses into her feelings.
- **Body Language Cues That Reveal Her True Feelings**
    - If you have the opportunity to see your ex in person, her body language can speak volumes:
- **Eye Contact:**
    - Prolonged eye contact suggests she's still attracted to you.
    - Avoiding eye contact could mean she's uncomfortable or trying to hide her emotions.
- **Physical Proximity:**
    - Standing close to you or finding reasons to touch you indicates she still feels a connection.
    - Maintaining physical distance might mean she's trying to establish boundaries.

PART 1: DECODING HER TRUE FEELINGS

- **Body Orientation:**
  - If her body is turned towards you while talking, she's engaged and interested.
  - Turning away or angling her body elsewhere suggests discomfort or a desire to leave.
- **Facial Expressions:**
  - Genuine smiles (look for crinkles around the eyes) show she's happy to see you.
  - Forced smiles or neutral expressions might indicate she's masking her true feelings.
- **Mirroring:**
  - If she unconsciously mimics your postures or gestures, it's a sign of rapport and attraction.
- **Nervous Behaviors:**
  - Playing with hair, fidgeting, or adjusting clothes can indicate she's nervous around you, which often suggests lingering feelings.
- **Tone of Voice:**
  - A softer, warmer tone when speaking to you (compared to others) suggests special feelings for you.
  - A flat or cold tone might indicate she's trying to maintain emotional distance.
- **Physical Barriers:**
  - Crossing arms or holding objects between you can be a subconscious way of creating distance.

Remember, no single cue is definitive. Look for patterns and clusters of behaviors to get a more accurate read on her feelings.

PART 1: DECODING HER TRUE FEELINGS

Also, be aware that she might be consciously trying to control her body language, especially if she knows you're observing her.

By mastering the art of decoding her messages, social media behavior, and body language, you'll gain valuable insights into her true feelings. This understanding is crucial for timing your actions correctly and choosing the right approach to reignite her interest in you.

PART 2:

The No-Contact Strategy That Drives Her Wild

21 Psychological Triggers to Make Her Beg You for a Second Chance

PART 2: THE NO-CONTACT STRATEGY THAT DRIVES HER WILD

Master the "No Contact Strategy"

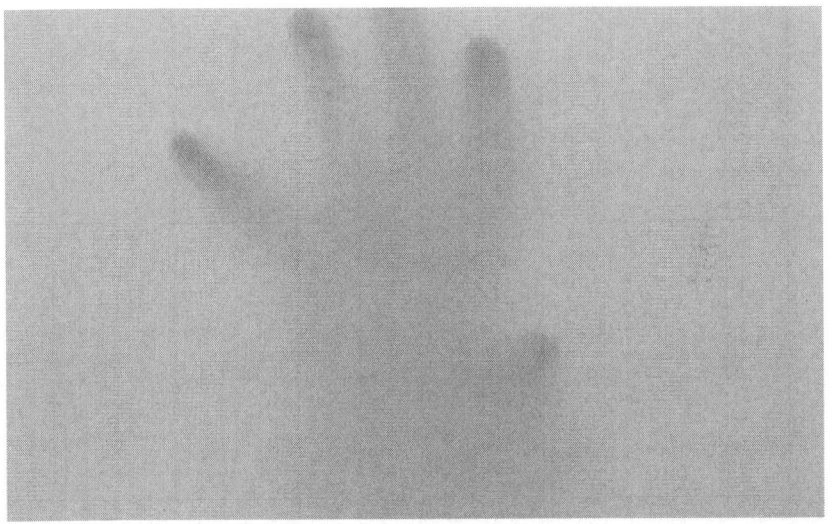

The No Contact Strategy is a powerful tool in your arsenal for winning back your ex. When implemented correctly, it can transform her indifference into intense longing. Let's dive into why this strategy works and how to use it effectively.

Why It Works and How to Implement It Correctly

The No Contact Strategy works on multiple psychological levels:

PART 2: THE NO-CONTACT STRATEGY THAT DRIVES HER WILD

- **It Triggers Loss Aversion:** Humans are wired to respond strongly to loss. When you suddenly disappear from her life, it creates a void that she can't help but notice. Even if she initiated the breakup, your absence will make her question her decision.
- **It Satisfies Her Need for Unpredictability:** By not reaching out when she expects you to, you become more interesting and mysterious. This unpredictability is crucial for rekindling attraction.
- **It Creates an Information Gap:** When you go silent, her mind starts filling in the blanks about what you're doing and why you're not contacting her. This mental engagement keeps you at the forefront of her thoughts.
- **It Raises Your Value Through Scarcity:** Absence truly does make the heart grow fonder. By making yourself scarce, you increase your perceived value in her eyes.
- **It Demonstrates Strength and Self-Respect:** Not contacting her shows that you have the emotional strength to walk away, which is inherently attractive to women.

How to Implement No Contact Correctly:
- **Commit to a Minimum of 30 Days:** The standard rule is 30 days of no contact. However, if you've been pleading or begging, you may need to extend this to 60 days or more.
- **Cut All Forms of Communication:** This means no calls, texts, emails, social media interactions, or "accidental" run-ins. You need to disappear completely from her life.

PART 2: THE NO-CONTACT STRATEGY THAT DRIVES HER WILD

- **Resist the Urge to Check Up on Her:** Don't stalk her social media or ask mutual friends about her. This period is about focusing on yourself.
- **Use This Time for Self-Improvement:** Work out, pursue hobbies, advance your career. Become the best version of yourself.
- **Don't Break No Contact, Even if She Reaches Out:** Unless it's an absolute emergency, maintain your silence even if she contacts you. This consistency is crucial for the strategy's effectiveness.
- **Prepare for the End of No Contact:** Plan how you'll re-establish contact in a way that showcases your growth and renewed confidence.

Turning Her Cold Silence into Desperate Longing
As you maintain No Contact, several psychological processes will work in your favor:

- **The Pendulum Effect:** Initially, she may feel relief at the breakup. But as time passes without hearing from you, her emotions will swing back towards missing you and questioning her decision.
- **Curiosity Builds**: Your silence will make her wonder what you're up to. Are you dating someone new? Have you moved on? This curiosity can drive her to reach out.
- **She'll Start to Idealize the Relationship:** Without your presence to remind her of any negatives, she'll begin to focus on the good times you shared.

PART 2: THE NO-CONTACT STRATEGY THAT DRIVES HER WILD

- **Fear of Loss Sets In:** As days pass without contact, she may start to worry that she's lost you for good. This fear can be a powerful motivator for her to reconnect.
- **She'll Question Her Decision:** Your silence gives her space to reflect on the breakup. Without you there trying to convince her otherwise, she may start to doubt whether ending things was the right choice.
- **Attraction Begins to Rebuild:** As she wonders about you and remembers the good times, her attraction to you will naturally start to increase.
- **She'll Start to Chase You:** If you've implemented No Contact correctly, there's a good chance she'll reach out to you before the 30 days are up.

Remember, the No Contact Strategy isn't about playing games or manipulating her. It's about giving both of you the space to heal, reflect, and grow. It allows her to miss you naturally, without feeling pressured or guilt-tripped.

By the end of the No Contact period, you'll be in a much stronger position to re-attract her. You'll have had time to work on yourself, and she'll have had time to process her emotions and realize what she's missing without you in her life.

In the next section, we'll explore how to use this period of silence to your advantage, focusing on self-improvement and subtle ways to showcase your growth, even while maintaining No Contact.

21 PSYCHOLOGICAL TRIGGERS TO MAKE YOUR EX BEG YOU FOR A SECOND CHANCE

PART 2: THE NO-CONTACT STRATEGY THAT DRIVES HER WILD

The Psychology of Scarcity
Understanding and leveraging the psychology of scarcity is crucial in your journey to win back your ex. This powerful principle can transform her indifference into intense desire, making her realize just how much she misses having you in her life.

Using Absence to Make Her Heart Grow Fonder
The concept of scarcity in relationships is rooted in basic human psychology. We tend to value what's rare or hard to obtain more than what's readily available. Here's how to use this to your advantage:

- **Create an Emotional Vacuum:** By removing yourself from her life completely, you create an emotional void. Nature abhors a vacuum, and she'll instinctively want to fill this void.
- **Activate Her Loss Aversion:** Humans are wired to be more motivated by the fear of loss than the prospect of gain. Your absence will trigger her fear of losing you permanently, even if she initiated the breakup.
- **Increase Your Perceived Value:** When you're constantly available, your value diminishes in her eyes. By becoming scarce, you instantly become more valuable and desirable.
- **Trigger Nostalgic Memories:** In your absence, she's more likely to remember the good times you shared, rather than focusing on the reasons for the breakup.

PART 2: THE NO-CONTACT STRATEGY THAT DRIVES HER WILD

- **Spark Her Curiosity:** Your sudden disappearance will make her wonder what you're doing, who you're with, and if you've moved on. This curiosity can be a powerful motivator for her to reach out.
- **Allow Her to Miss You:** It's impossible for her to miss you if you're always around or in contact. Absence gives her the opportunity to genuinely long for your presence.
- **Demonstrate Your Independence:** Showing that you can live a fulfilling life without her challenges any assumptions she might have had about your dependency on the relationship.

Implementing Scarcity:
- **Maintain Strict No Contact:** This means no calls, texts, emails, or social media interaction.
- **Avoid Mutual Hangouts:** Don't frequent places you know she'll be.
- **Limit Information Flow:** Don't update mutual friends about your life in ways that will get back to her.

The Pendulum Effect: Swinging Her Emotions in Your Favor
The Pendulum Effect is a powerful psychological phenomenon that occurs during the No Contact period. Understanding and leveraging this effect can significantly increase your chances of rekindling her interest.

How the Pendulum Effect Works:

21 PSYCHOLOGICAL TRIGGERS TO MAKE YOUR EX BEG YOU FOR A SECOND CHANCE

PART 2: THE NO-CONTACT STRATEGY THAT DRIVES HER WILD

- **Initial Relief:** Immediately after the breakup, she may feel a sense of relief. This is especially true if the relationship had been stressful or if she had been contemplating the breakup for a while.
- **Doubt Creeps In:** As days pass without hearing from you, she'll start to wonder why you haven't reached out. This plants the seed of doubt about her decision.
- **Curiosity Grows:** Her mind will start to wander. What are you doing? Have you moved on? Are you dating someone new? This curiosity will keep you in her thoughts.
- **Negative Memories Fade:** With time and distance, the negative aspects of your relationship that led to the breakup will begin to fade from her memory.
- **Positive Memories Intensify:** In contrast, she'll start to focus more on the good times you shared. These positive memories will become more vivid and frequent.
- **Fear of Loss Intensifies:** As more time passes, she'll start to worry that she might have lost you for good. This fear can be a powerful motivator.
- **Idealization:** In your absence, she may start to idealize you and the relationship, remembering only the best parts.
- **Longing Develops:** Eventually, the pendulum swings fully in your favor. She'll start to miss you intensely and long for your presence in her life.

Maximizing the Pendulum Effect:

PART 2: THE NO-CONTACT STRATEGY THAT DRIVES HER WILD

- **Patience is Crucial:** The full swing of the pendulum can take time. Don't rush the process.
- **Subtle Social Media Updates:** If you're connected on social media, occasional posts showing you living your best life can amplify the effect.
- **Focus on Self-Improvement:** The more you improve yourself during this time, the more powerful the pendulum swing will be when she finally sees or hears from you again.
- **Prepare for Contact:** When you do finally break the silence, be ready to present the best version of yourself.

Remember, the Pendulum Effect is not about manipulation. It's about giving her the space and time to naturally reevaluate the relationship and her feelings for you. By understanding and respecting this process, you set the stage for a potential reconciliation based on genuine emotions rather than guilt or pressure.

In the next section, we'll explore how to effectively use social media during the No Contact period to subtly showcase your growth and keep her intrigued without directly engaging with her.

Social Media Secrets
In today's digital age, social media plays a crucial role in how we perceive and interact with others. When used strategically, it can be a powerful tool in rekindling your ex's interest.

PART 2: THE NO-CONTACT STRATEGY THAT DRIVES HER WILD

Let's explore how to craft an online presence that subtly showcases your value and makes her green with envy, all without looking like you're trying.

Crafting an Online Presence That Subtly Showcases Your Value

- **Update Your Profile:** Start by refreshing your profile pictures and information. Choose photos that show you at your best – confident, happy, and engaged in interesting activities. This immediate visual change will catch her attention.
- **Quality Over Quantity:** Don't flood your feed with posts. Instead, focus on sharing high-quality content that reflects positively on you. This could include:
    - Photos of you enjoying new hobbies
    - Updates about career achievements
    - Pictures with friends and family
- **Demonstrate Personal Growth:** Share content that shows you're working on self-improvement. This might include:
    - Books you're reading
    - New skills you're learning
    - Fitness goals you're achieving
- **Showcase Your Social Life:** Post photos of you out with friends or at social events. This shows you're not sitting at home pining for her, but living a full, enjoyable life.
- **Highlight Your Achievements:** Don't be afraid to share your successes, whether they're professional or personal. This builds your perceived value.

PART 2: THE NO-CONTACT STRATEGY THAT DRIVES HER WILD

Making Her Green With Envy (Without Looking Like You're Trying)

The key here is subtlety. You want to create a sense of FOMO (Fear of Missing Out) without appearing like you're deliberately trying to make her jealous.

- **The "Accidental" Glimpse:** Post photos that give a tantalizing glimpse into your life, like a dinner table set for two, or a woman's hand in the corner of a photo. This sparks curiosity without explicitly showing you're dating.
- **Leverage Mutual Friends:** If you're out with mutual friends, let them post the photos instead of you. This seems more natural and less like you're trying to show off.
- **Location Tags:** Check in at interesting locations – new restaurants, travel destinations, or events she might wish she was attending with you.
- **Subtle Hints at Dating:** Without explicitly mentioning dating, post content that suggests you might be. For example, a photo captioned "Great night out!" at a romantic restaurant.
- **Showcase New Interests:** Post about new hobbies or activities, especially ones she might have wanted you to try during your relationship. This shows growth and may make her regret not being part of your journey.
- **Use Humor:** Funny posts or memes can make you seem upbeat and attractive. If you can reference inside jokes or shared experiences subtly, even better.

PART 2: THE NO-CONTACT STRATEGY THAT DRIVES HER WILD

- **Timing is Everything:** Post during times she's likely to be online, increasing the chances she'll see your updates in real-time.
- **The "Moving On" Vibe:** Occasionally post philosophical or positive quotes about personal growth, new beginnings, or finding happiness. This suggests you're emotionally moving forward.
- **Mutual Interest Engagement:** Comment on or share content related to interests you shared. This reminds her of your connection without directly engaging with her.
- **The Unexpected Skill:** Share updates about learning a new skill she wouldn't expect – like cooking, a new language, or an instrument. This intrigues her and shows personal development.

Remember, the goal is not to make her feel bad or to play games. It's about presenting an authentic, improved version of yourself that naturally draws her interest. Your social media should reflect genuine positive changes in your life, not a fabricated image.

Avoid These Pitfalls:
- Don't overdo it. Posting too frequently or too many "look how great I am" posts will seem desperate or inauthentic.
- Never post anything negative about her or the relationship.
- Avoid obvious attempts to make her jealous, like posting photos with other women.

PART 2: THE NO-CONTACT STRATEGY THAT DRIVES HER WILD

- Don't drunk post or share content that reflects poorly on you.

By mastering these social media strategies, you create an image of a man who's thriving post-breakup. This not only increases your chances of rekindling her interest but also genuinely improves your life and mindset.

In the next section, we'll explore how to interpret her social media behavior and use it to gauge her emotional state and interest level in you.

21 PSYCHOLOGICAL TRIGGERS TO MAKE YOUR EX BEG YOU FOR A SECOND CHANCE

PART 3: REIGNITING HER ATTRACTION

- **The Scarcity Principle:** Humans value what's rare or difficult to obtain. By making yourself less available, you increase your perceived value in her eyes. This doesn't mean playing games, but rather focusing on your own life and passions.
    - Implementation:
        - Maintain the No Contact rule religiously
        - When you do reconnect, keep conversations brief and end them first
        - Don't always be available when she reaches out

- **The Rekindled Memories Technique:** Positive memories associated with you can trigger strong emotions and longing.
    - Implementation:
        - Subtly remind her of good times you shared without explicitly mentioning them
        - Use inside jokes or references to past experiences in casual conversation
        - Share photos on social media that might remind her of happy moments with you
- **The Confidence Revival System:** Confidence is incredibly attractive. By rebuilding your self-assurance, you become more appealing not just to her, but to everyone around you.
    - Implementation:
        - Focus on self-improvement: fitness, career, hobbies
        - Practice positive self-talk and affirmations
        - Set and achieve personal goals

PART 3: REIGNITING HER ATTRACTION

- **The Jealousy Switch:** While you shouldn't play childish games, a little bit of jealousy can reignite her competitive instincts and make her see you as a prize to be won.
    - Implementation:
        - Casually mention new friends or social activities
        - Allow her to see (through social media or mutual friends) that you're living an exciting life
        - Don't hide the fact that other women find you attractive
- **Future Projection:** Paint a vivid picture of an attractive future that subtly includes her, making her yearn to be part of it.
    - Implementation:
        - Share your ambitious plans and goals
        - Talk about exciting future events or trips
        - Describe positive changes you're making in your life
- **The Emotional Time Machine:** Transport her back to the emotional state she was in when she first fell for you.
    - Implementation:
        - Recreate elements of your early dating phase (e.g., revisit old date spots)
        - Embody the qualities that initially attracted her to you
        - Use similar language or gestures from when you first started dating

Becoming the Man She Can't Stop Thinking About

PART 3: REIGNITING HER ATTRACTION

To truly become irresistible to your ex, you need to transform into the best version of yourself. Here's how:

- **Embrace Personal Growth:** Show her that you're constantly evolving and improving. This creates intrigue and respect.
    - Learn new skills or hobbies
    - Read widely and be able to discuss interesting topics
    - Set ambitious goals and work towards them
- **Master Emotional Intelligence:** Women are attracted to men who understand and can manage their emotions.
    - Practice active listening
    - Show empathy in your interactions
    - Learn to express your feelings maturely
- **Cultivate Mystery:** Don't be an open book. A little mystery keeps her thinking about you.
    - Don't overshare on social media
    - Keep some aspects of your life private
    - Be unpredictable (in a positive way)
- **Demonstrate High Value:** Showcase the qualities that make you a catch without bragging.
    - Let your actions speak louder than words
    - Surround yourself with quality people
    - Achieve things that you're proud of
- **Master the Art of Subtle Flirting:** When you do interact, keep things light and playful.
    - Use gentle teasing
    - Maintain strong eye contact
    - Use light, appropriate touch when in person

PART 3: REIGNITING HER ATTRACTION

- **The "Misattribution of Arousal":** This phenomenon occurs when people mistakenly attribute their physiological response to the wrong source. Here's how to use it:
    - Engage in exciting activities: When you do meet, choose activities that get the heart racing (e.g., amusement parks, sports).
    - Create situations of mild anxiety or excitement: These feelings can be misattributed as attraction.

- **The "Pratfall Effect":** This effect suggests that people who are competent but make occasional minor mistakes are more likeable and attractive. To implement:
    - Show vulnerability: Share a minor flaw or mistake, but handle it with grace and humor.
    - Don't try to be perfect: Allow her to see that you're human, which makes you more relatable and attractive.

- **The "Reciprocal Liking" Principle:** People tend to like those who they believe like them. Use this subtly:
    - Give genuine compliments: Notice and appreciate positive changes in her.
    - Show interest in her growth: Express admiration for her achievements or new skills.

- **The "Mere Exposure Effect":** This psychological phenomenon states that people tend to develop a preference for things merely because they are familiar with them. To leverage this:

PART 3: REIGNITING HER ATTRACTION

- Increase non-intrusive exposure: Frequent places she might be, without directly interacting.
- Maintain a consistent online presence: Regular, positive social media updates can keep you in her thoughts.

- **Creating Cognitive Dissonance:** This occurs when a person holds contradictory beliefs or ideas. Use it to challenge her indifference:
    - Behave contrary to her expectations: If she expects you to be upset, be cheerful and unbothered.
    - Show growth in areas she criticized: If she thought you were irresponsible, demonstrate your new-found reliability.

- **The "Scarcity-Reactance" Combo:** Combine the scarcity principle with psychological reactance (people's tendency to do the opposite of what they're told):
    - Limit your availability, but don't forbid contact: This creates a desire to reach out.
    - Suggest she might not be ready for the new you: This can trigger her desire to prove otherwise.

By implementing these advanced psychological techniques, you create an environment where her indifference naturally evolves into curiosity and desire. Remember, the key is subtlety and authenticity. These methods work best when they're a natural extension of your genuine self-improvement journey.

PART 3: REIGNITING HER ATTRACTION

The Confidence Revival System
After a breakup, many men experience a significant blow to their self-esteem. This system is designed to help you rebuild your confidence in the context of your recent heartbreak.

Eliminating Post-Breakup Insecurities
- **Confront the "Not Good Enough" Mindset:** It's common to feel like you weren't "enough" for your ex. Challenge this by:
    - Listing specific qualities your ex appreciated about you
    - Reminding yourself that compatibility issues don't equate to personal failings
    - Recognizing that one person's opinion doesn't define your worth
- **Address Feelings of Rejection:**
    - Understand that her leaving doesn't diminish your value as a man
    - Reframe the breakup as a mismatch rather than a personal failure
    - Remind yourself of past successes in other areas of life
- **Combat Comparison Anxiety:** If you're worried she'll find someone "better," remember:
    - Your unique qualities can't be replicated or replaced
    - Focus on becoming the best version of yourself, not competing with imaginary rivals
    - Recognize that the "grass is greener" mentality is often an illusion

PART 3: REIGNITING HER ATTRACTION

- **Tackle the Fear of Being Alone:**
    - Engage in activities you couldn't or didn't do while in the relationship
    - Reconnect with male friends for support and camaraderie
    - Use this time to rediscover your individual identity outside of the relationship
- **Overcome Performance Anxiety:** If you're worried about future relationships:
    - Remind yourself of positive experiences from your past
    - Focus on personal growth rather than trying to be "perfect" for someone else
    - Recognize that vulnerability and authenticity are strengths, not weaknesses

Projecting Unshakeable Self-Assurance (Post-Breakup Edition)

- **Embrace the "Blank Slate" Mentality:** See this as an opportunity to reinvent yourself. Your ex's departure doesn't define your future.
- **Reclaim Your Personal Power:**
    - Make decisions that you may have compromised on during the relationship
    - Set new personal goals that are entirely your own
    - Take control of your daily routine and living space

PART 3: REIGNITING HER ATTRACTION

- **Showcase Your Resilience:**
    - If you encounter mutual friends, project a positive attitude
    - Demonstrate through actions that you're moving forward, not dwelling in the past
    - Take on new challenges to prove to yourself that you can overcome adversity
- **Redefine Your Social Value:**
    - Engage in group activities where you can demonstrate leadership or skill
    - Share your knowledge or expertise in areas you're passionate about
    - Be the supportive friend others can rely on, boosting your sense of worth
- **Own Your Emotional Journey:**
    - Acknowledge your pain without shame – it shows you're capable of deep feelings
    - Share your experience of growth with others when appropriate
    - Use humor to show you can find light even in difficult situations
- **Physical Presence Makeover:**
    - Stand tall and move with purpose – your body language should say "I'm moving forward"
    - Make eye contact confidently, especially if you encounter your ex
    - Speak clearly and avoid nervous habits like fidgeting or looking down

PART 3: REIGNITING HER ATTRACTION

- **Develop a "Been There, Done That" Attitude:**
    - Reflect on how you've grown from the relationship and breakup
    - Recognize that you now have valuable experience that makes you a more understanding partner
    - Project the quiet confidence of someone who's faced heartbreak and come out stronger

Remember, rebuilding confidence after a breakup is a process. It's okay to have moments of doubt, but consistently applying these strategies will help you emerge as a stronger, more self-assured man - one who's even more attractive than before.

In the next section, we'll explore how to channel this newfound confidence into becoming the type of man your ex can't help but be drawn to once again.

The Masculine Metamorphosis
When you're reeling from a breakup, it's easy to lose sight of your masculine essence. However, reclaiming and enhancing your masculinity is crucial in reigniting your ex's attraction. This section will guide you through embodying the strong, decisive man she craves while striking the perfect balance of strength and sensitivity.

Embodying the Strong, Decisive Man She Craves
- Embrace Your Primal Nature: Women are biologically wired to be attracted to men who exhibit strong, masculine traits.

PART 3: REIGNITING HER ATTRACTION

- This doesn't mean becoming a caricature of masculinity, but rather tapping into your innate male energy.
    - Engage in physical activities that boost testosterone, like weightlifting or competitive sports
    - Practice deep, controlled breathing to lower your voice naturally
    - Stand tall with your shoulders back and chin slightly raised
- **Cultivate Decisiveness:** Indecision is a major turn-off. Start making choices quickly and confidently, even in small matters.
    - When planning activities, propose specific ideas rather than asking "What do you want to do?"
    - Make reservations or arrangements without seeking approval
    - When asked for your opinion, give it directly without hedging
- **Develop Unshakeable Frame:** Your "frame" is your perspective on the world. A strong frame is attractive because it shows you're grounded in your beliefs and values.
    - Define your core values and stick to them, even in the face of opposition
    - Practice staying calm and composed during heated discussions
    - Learn to respectfully disagree without becoming defensive or aggressive

PART 3: REIGNITING HER ATTRACTION

- **Master the Art of Leading:** Leadership is an attractive quality that demonstrates competence and reliability.
    - Take charge in group situations by organizing events or activities
    - Be the one to make decisions when others are hesitant
    - Offer guidance and support to those around you, showcasing your ability to lead
- **Cultivate Mystery and Unpredictability:** While reliability is important, being too predictable can dampen attraction. Inject some mystery into your persona.
    - Develop new skills or hobbies that she doesn't know about
    - Plan surprising and exciting activities
    - Maintain some privacy about your personal life, leaving her curious to know more
- **Striking the Right Balance of Strength and Sensitivity**
    - While embodying masculine strength is crucial, it's equally important to balance this with emotional intelligence and sensitivity. Here's how to strike that balance:
- **Practice Controlled Vulnerability:** Show that you're capable of opening up emotionally, but do so strategically.
    - Share personal stories that reveal your depth, but avoid oversharing or seeming needy
    - Express your feelings clearly and concisely, without expecting her to "fix" them
    - Demonstrate that you're comfortable with your emotions without being ruled by them

PART 3: REIGNITING HER ATTRACTION

- **Develop Empathetic Listening:** Show that you can be both strong and understanding by mastering the art of empathetic listening.
    - Give her your full attention when she's speaking
    - Validate her feelings without immediately trying to solve her problems
    - Ask insightful questions that show you're truly interested in her perspective
- **Show Protective Instincts Without Possessiveness:** Tap into the primal female desire for a protector without being controlling.
    - Offer your jacket when it's cold without insisting if she declines
    - Walk on the street side of the sidewalk
    - Show concern for her safety and well-being without being overbearing
- **Demonstrate Emotional Stability:** Prove that you can be her rock during turbulent times.
    - Stay calm and composed during stressful situations
    - Offer support and reassurance when she's facing challenges
    - Avoid dramatic emotional displays or outbursts
- **Balance Assertiveness with Respect:** Show that you can stand up for yourself and others without being aggressive.
    - Clearly state your boundaries and expectations
    - Defend your beliefs and values confidently, but respect others' right to disagree
    - Stand up against injustice or disrespect, but do so calmly and rationally

PART 3: REIGNITING HER ATTRACTION

- **Cultivate Gentle Strength:** Demonstrate that true strength lies in gentleness and self-control.
    - Be kind and patient with children, animals, and those weaker than you
    - Show restraint in your physical strength, using it only when necessary
    - Be the calm in the storm during chaotic or emotional situations
- **Master the Art of Playful Teasing:** Use humor and light-hearted teasing to create emotional spikes without being hurtful.
    - Gently tease her about quirks or habits you find endearing
    - Use playful nicknames that highlight positive aspects of her personality
    - Engage in witty banter that challenges her intellectually

By mastering these aspects of masculine metamorphosis, you'll become the kind of man your ex can't help but be drawn to. Remember, this isn't about changing who you are at your core, but rather about enhancing your natural masculine traits while developing emotional intelligence.

In the next section, we'll explore how to use these newly developed qualities to create an irresistible future vision that will make her desperate to be a part of your life again.

PART 4:

Erasing the Competition

21 Psychological Triggers to Make Her
Beg You for a Second Chance

PART 4: ERASING THE COMPETITION

Erase the "Other Guy" from Her Mind

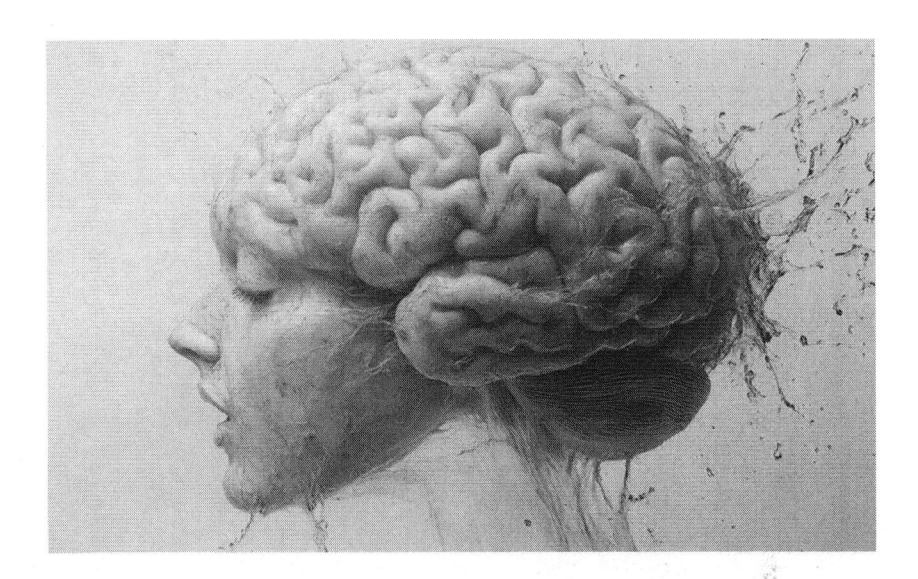

When your ex is seeing someone new, it can feel devastating. However, with the right strategy, you can still outshine any competition and regain her interest. Outshining any competition, even if she's seeing someone new

- **Focus on Self-Improvement:** Instead of directly competing, become the best version of yourself.
    - Set and achieve ambitious personal goals
    - Develop new skills that align with your passions
    - Transform your physique through dedicated fitness regimes

21 PSYCHOLOGICAL TRIGGERS TO MAKE YOUR EX BEG YOU FOR A SECOND CHANCE

PART 4: ERASING THE COMPETITION

- **Cultivate an Abundance Mindset:** Show her that your worth isn't dependent on her or any relationship.
    - Expand your social circle with high-quality friends
    - Pursue exciting hobbies and interests
    - Demonstrate success in your career or personal projects
- **Master Emotional Control:** Show that you're emotionally stable and mature, unlike most men after a breakup.
    - Maintain composure in all interactions, especially if you encounter her
    - Avoid showing jealousy or bitterness about her new relationship
    - Respond to any provocations with calm assurance
- **Leverage Mutual Connections Wisely:** Use your shared social network to your advantage, without being manipulative.
    - Be the life of the party at social gatherings she might hear about
    - Cultivate stronger relationships with mutual friends
    - Let your positive changes naturally filter back to her through others
- **Redefine Your Image:** Present a new, improved version of yourself that she can't ignore.
    - Update your style to reflect your personal growth
    - Engage in activities that showcase your adventurous side
    - Share your new outlook on life through social media, without targeting her

PART 4: ERASING THE COMPETITION

The Comparison Trigger: Making other men pale in comparison

- **Amplify Your Unique Qualities:** Emphasize the traits that set you apart from other men, especially her new partner.
    - Showcase your special talents or skills
    - Highlight the qualities she once admired in you
    - Demonstrate growth in areas where you previously fell short
- **Showcase Emotional Intelligence:** Display a level of emotional depth that's rare and attractive.
    - If you cross paths, show genuine interest in her growth and well-being
    - Demonstrate empathy and understanding in your interactions with others
    - Handle difficult situations with grace and maturity
- **Exhibit Leadership and Decision-Making:** Women are attracted to men who can take charge and make decisions.
    - Take initiative in group settings
    - Share stories of how you've successfully navigated challenges
    - Demonstrate confidence in your choices and actions
- **Display Ambition and Drive:** Show that you're a man with a vision and the determination to achieve it.
    - Share your ambitious goals and the steps you're taking to achieve them

PART 4: ERASING THE COMPETITION

- Demonstrate passion and dedication in your pursuits
- Let it be known that you're constantly striving for self-improvement
- **Cultivate an Aura of Mystery:** Pique her curiosity by becoming more intriguing and less predictable.
  - Be selective about what you share on social media
  - Engage in new, unexpected activities that she might hear about
  - Maintain an air of quiet confidence about your personal life
- **Demonstrate High Value Through Actions:** Let your behavior and achievements speak louder than words.
  - Achieve notable successes in your career or personal projects
  - Be seen as someone who adds value to others' lives
- **Master the Art of Subtle Charm:** If you do interact, leave a lasting positive impression.
  - Use humor and wit to create enjoyable interactions
  - Show genuine interest in others, not just her
  - Leave conversations on a high note, making others (including her) want more

By implementing these strategies, you're not directly competing with her new partner. Instead, you're becoming a man of such high value that she can't help but question her current choice. Remember, the goal is to focus on your own growth and let her naturally recognize your enhanced value.

PART 4: ERASING THE COMPETITION

In the next section, we'll explore how to make her jealous in a way that amplifies her attraction without resorting to childish games or manipulation.

Discover How to Make Her Jealous

Activating her possessive instincts without childish games

1. The "Phantom Ex" Technique:
   - Create an air of mystery around your dating life
   - When she or mutual friends inquire, respond with a knowing smile and change the subject
   - Let her imagination run wild about the possibilities
- The "Skill Acquisition Sprint":
   - Rapidly develop a new, impressive skill she always wished you had (e.g., cooking, dancing, speaking a new language)
   - Showcase this skill subtly in social situations or through mutual friends
   - Let her wonder why you've suddenly become so motivated to improve yourself
- The "Happiness Paradox":
   - Genuinely focus on your own joy and fulfillment, independent of relationships
   - Share moments of pure, unadulterated happiness on social media or through mutual friends
   - Make her question why you seem happier without her

PART 4: ERASING THE COMPETITION

- **The "Selective Memory" Approach:**
    - When reminiscing with mutual friends, only bring up positive memories that don't involve her
    - Create the impression that your best times were outside of your relationship with her
    - Make her feel like she's missing out on the "real you"
- The "Passion Project" Reveal:
    - Immerse yourself in a challenging, impressive project you've always talked about but never started
    - Share updates on your progress, showcasing your dedication and growth
    - Let her see the driven, passionate side of you that she may have forgotten

Using social proof to your advantage
- **The "Social Circle Upgrade":**
    - Cultivate friendships with people she's always admired or wanted to know
    - Become the connector in your social group, the one who knows everyone
    - Make her realize that being with you means access to an exciting, elevated social life
- **The "Admiration Accumulation":**
    - Collect genuine compliments and admiration from others, especially those she respects
    - Have these praises casually mentioned to her by mutual friends
    - Create an aura of being universally adored and respected

PART 4: ERASING THE COMPETITION

- **The "Unexpected Ally" Maneuver:**
    - Befriend someone she never thought would like you (e.g., a critical family member, a friend who was skeptical of you)
    - Let her hear about how this person now sings your praises
    - Make her question her own judgment about you
- **The "Social Media Illusion":**
    - Curate your social media to showcase a life that's exciting, but just believable enough
    - Use strategic posting times when she's most likely to be online
    - Create FOMO (Fear of Missing Out) without directly interacting with her
- **The "Mutual Friend Makeover":**
    - Significantly improve your relationship with a mutual friend she's close to
    - Become this friend's go-to person for advice, fun, or support
    - Let her see how valued you are by someone whose opinion she trusts

By implementing these strategies, you're not just making her jealous – you're transforming her entire perception of you. You're becoming the man she always wished you could be, and more importantly, the man she fears losing to someone else. This isn't about playing games; it's about genuine self-improvement and social elevation that naturally triggers her jealousy and re-attraction.

PART 4: ERASING THE COMPETITION

Remember, the goal is to make her regret her decision to leave, not out of spite, but because she's realizing the incredible value you bring to her life. As she sees you thriving and becoming increasingly desirable to others, her possessive instincts will kick in, making her want to reclaim what she now perceives as rightfully hers – you.

The Value Elevator
When you're desperate to win her back, you need to drastically elevate your perceived value in her eyes. This isn't about superficial changes; it's about becoming the man she can't resist. Here's how to skyrocket your worth and make other guys seem utterly dull in comparison.

Instantly boosting your perceived value in her eyes

- **The "Reality Show Transformation":**
    - Undergo a dramatic physical transformation in a short period
    - Document your journey on social media, showing before and after photos
    - Ensure mutual friends mention your incredible change to her
- **The "Bucket List Blitz":**
    - Tackle your most ambitious bucket list items aggressively
    - Share these experiences through vivid storytelling with mutual friends
    - Create an image of a man living life to the fullest, making her wonder why she's missing out

PART 4: ERASING THE COMPETITION

- **The "Entrepreneurial Explosion":**
    - Start a side business or project that aligns with your passions
    - Let news of your venture's success spread through your social circle
    - Become known as the guy who's not just dreaming, but doing
- **The "Intellectual Insurgence":**
    - Dive deep into complex, fascinating topics she's interested in
    - Casually display your new knowledge in group settings
    - Become the go-to person for intriguing conversations, outshining her current partner
- **The "Humanitarian Hero":**
    - Engage in meaningful volunteer work or start a charitable initiative
    - Ensure your efforts get local recognition or press coverage
    - Let her see you as someone making a real difference in the world
    - Making other guys seem boring in comparison
- **The "Adventure Architect":**
    - Plan and execute extraordinary adventures that push your limits
    - Share thrilling stories and photos that make everyday life seem pale in comparison
    - Become known as the guy who always has an incredible experience to share

PART 4: ERASING THE COMPETITION

- **The "Social Chameleon":**
  - Develop the ability to fit in and thrive in diverse social settings
  - Showcase your versatility by excelling in various environments she frequents
  - Make her current partner seem one-dimensional in comparison
- **The "Passion Polymath":**
  - Cultivate multiple, unusual passions and skills
  - Demonstrate your diverse talents in social settings
  - Create an image of a Renaissance man that leaves others seeming mundane
- **The "Emotional Alchemist":**
  - Master the art of creating intense, positive emotions in others
  - Become known for your ability to turn any situation into a memorable experience
  - Make her realize that life without you lacks color and excitement
- **The "Future Visionary":**
  - Develop and articulate an inspiring vision for your future
  - Share your plans in a way that makes others want to be part of your journey
  - Make her question whether her current path is as exciting as the one you're on

By implementing these strategies, you're not just improving yourself; you're becoming a man of exceptional value. You're creating a life so vibrant and compelling that she can't help but be drawn back to you.

PART 4: ERASING THE COMPETITION

This isn't about comparison or competition; it's about becoming the best version of yourself – a version so remarkable that she'll question how she ever let you go.

Remember, this transformation is not just for her. It's about becoming a man of high value in every aspect of life. As you elevate yourself, you'll find that not only will she be irresistibly attracted to you, but you'll also open doors to opportunities and experiences you never thought possible.

In the next section, we'll explore how to use this newfound value to reignite her emotional connection and make her burn with desire for you once again.

PART 5:

Reigniting Her Emotional Hot Buttons

21 Psychological Triggers to Make Her Beg You for a Second Chance

21 PSYCHOLOGICAL TRIGGERS TO MAKE YOUR EX BEG YOU FOR A SECOND CHANCE

PART 5: REIGNITING HER EMOTIONAL HOT BUTTONS

The Emotional Time Machine

When you're desperate to win her back, you need to tap into the powerful emotions she once felt for you. The Emotional Time Machine is a set of techniques designed to transport her back to the height of her feelings for you, making her question why she ever let you go.

Transporting her back to when she was madly in love with you
- The "Sensory Trigger Ambush":
    - Identify the specific cologne you wore during your happiest times together

PART 5: REIGNITING HER EMOTIONAL HOT BUTTONS

- ○ Wear it when you know you'll cross paths with her
- ○ The scent will instantly flood her with positive memories of you
- **The "Music Memory Hack":**
  - ○ Create a playlist of songs that were significant during your relationship's best moments
  - ○ Ensure these songs play in the background when you're in shared spaces
  - ○ Let the music subconsciously transport her to happier times with you
- **The "Photo Time Capsule":**
  - ○ Unearth a forgotten photo of a peak moment in your relationship
  - ○ "Accidentally" let her see it, perhaps by asking a mutual friend about the event in the photo
  - ○ Watch as the visual reminder triggers a flood of positive emotions
- **The "Taste of Love":**
  - ○ Recreate a meal or drink that was significant in your relationship
  - ○ Share it with mutual friends, ensuring she hears about it
  - ○ The taste and smell will evoke powerful memories of your time together
- **The "Landmark Love Reminder":**
  - ○ Casually mention or be seen at locations that hold special significance in your relationship
  - ○ Let her imagination run wild with memories of the moments you shared there
  - ○ Create a sense of nostalgia that makes her long for those times again

PART 5: REIGNITING HER EMOTIONAL HOT BUTTONS

Rekindling positive memories and peak experiences

- **The "Peak Moment Replay":**
    - Identify the absolute best moments of your relationship
    - Find subtle ways to recreate elements of these moments in your current interactions
    - Trigger her subconscious to associate you with those peak experiences
- **The "Laughter Flashback":**
    - Recall inside jokes or hilarious moments you shared
    - Find opportunities to reference these in group settings
    - Remind her of the unique connection and joy you brought to her life
- **The "Growth Together Reminder":**
    - Highlight how you've both grown since your relationship, but in ways you discussed together
    - Show her that you've become the man she always believed you could be
    - Make her feel that your growth journey isn't complete without her
- **The "Unfinished Bucket List":**
    - Bring up exciting plans or dreams you had together that weren't fulfilled
    - Casually mention how you're still interested in those experiences
    - Plant the seed that your best adventures together are still ahead

PART 5: REIGNITING HER EMOTIONAL HOT BUTTONS

- **The "Emotional Support Callback":**
    - Remind her of times when you were her rock during difficult moments
    - Subtly demonstrate that you still possess those supportive qualities
    - Make her question if she'll ever find that level of understanding and support again
- **The "Passion Reignition":**
    - Recreate elements of your most passionate moments, without being explicit
    - Use subtle touches, glances, or words that echo your most intimate times
    - Reignite the physical attraction by reminding her body of your connection
- **The "Future Echo":**
    - Reference future plans you had made together, as if they're still possible
    - Show her that the future she once dreamed of with you is still within reach
    - Make her realize that leaving you meant leaving behind a promising future

By masterfully employing these Emotional Time Machine techniques, you're not just reminding her of the past – you're making her feel those intense emotions all over again. You're showing her that the man she fell madly in love with isn't just a memory, but a reality she can have again.

PART 5: REIGNITING HER EMOTIONAL HOT BUTTONS

Remember, the goal isn't to live in the past, but to use those powerful positive memories as a bridge to a new, even better future together. As you trigger these emotional flashbacks, you're also demonstrating how you've grown and improved, creating an irresistible combination of familiar comfort and exciting potential.

In the next section, we'll explore how to use curiosity loops to keep her thinking about you constantly, even when she's trying to move on.

Curiosity Loops
When you're desperate to get your ex back, you need to become the puzzle she can't stop trying to solve. Curiosity loops are psychological triggers that keep her mind constantly returning to thoughts of you, even when she's trying to move on. Here's how to become her most intriguing obsession.

Keeping her thinking about you constantly

- **The "Cliffhanger Conversation":**
    - During interactions, start telling an exciting story about your life
    - Just as you reach the most interesting part, find a reason to leave
    - She'll be dying to know the end, ensuring she seeks you out again

PART 5: REIGNITING HER EMOTIONAL HOT BUTTONS

- **The "Mysterious Package":**
  - Send her a small, mysterious gift with no explanation
  - Choose something that relates to an inside joke or shared memory
  - Include only your initials, leaving her to wonder about your intentions
- **The "Social Media Blackout":**
  - Suddenly go completely dark on all social media platforms
  - After a week or two, post a single cryptic message or photo
  - Let her imagination run wild about what's happening in your life
- **The "Overheard Success":**
  - Arrange for her to overhear news of a major positive change in your life (new job, unexpected opportunity)
  - Ensure the information is vague and lacks details
  - She'll be curious to know more, potentially reaching out to you directly
- **The "Incomplete Transformation":**
  - Make a noticeable change to your appearance or behavior
  - When she or others comment, hint that it's part of a bigger change you're undergoing
  - Don't elaborate, leaving her curious about what else is changing in your life

PART 5: REIGNITING HER EMOTIONAL HOT BUTTONS

The art of mystery and intrigue

- **The "Selective Sharing" Technique:**
    - When talking to mutual friends, share exciting news but leave out key details
    - Ensure these friends mention your news to her, but can't satisfy her curiosity
    - She'll be compelled to reach out to you to get the full story
- **The "Cryptic Social Circle":**
    - Start spending time with a new group of interesting people
    - Ensure she hears about this through mutual friends, but don't explain who these people are
    - She'll be intrigued by the new connections you're making
- **The "Alternate Timeline" Hint:**
    - Casually mention to mutual friends a major life decision you're considering
    - Make it something unexpected that she wouldn't associate with you
    - She'll be curious about this potential new direction in your life
- **The "Unseen Growth" Strategy:**
    - Make significant personal improvements, but don't showcase them publicly
    - Let subtle hints of your growth slip out in conversations with mutual friends
    - She'll be intrigued by the changes she's hearing about but can't see

PART 5: REIGNITING HER EMOTIONAL HOT BUTTONS

- **The "Paradoxical Behavior" Tactic:**
    - Act in ways that seem contradictory to your usual behavior, but don't explain why
    - For example, if you were always career-focused, hint at taking time off for a secret project
    - She'll be puzzled by this new side of you, wanting to understand the change
- **The "Unfinished Story" Method:**
    - Start sharing a personal anecdote with mutual friends when she's present
    - As the story gets interesting, find a reason to stop abruptly
    - She'll be left wanting to hear the rest, potentially seeking you out to finish it

By implementing these curiosity loops, you're not just keeping yourself in her thoughts – you're becoming her most intriguing mystery. You're transforming from the ex she thought she knew into an enigma she's desperate to figure out.

Remember, the key is to provide just enough information to pique her interest, but never enough to satisfy her curiosity completely. Each loop should lead to another question in her mind, creating a chain of thoughts that always lead back to you.

PART 5: REIGNITING HER EMOTIONAL HOT BUTTONS

As she becomes more and more intrigued, she'll find herself thinking about you constantly, wondering about the changes in your life, and questioning her decision to end the relationship. This constant presence in her thoughts will reignite her emotional connection to you, making her increasingly eager to reconnect and discover the new, mysterious you.

In the next section, we'll explore how to use the "Obsession Formula" to turn her rekindled interest into an overwhelming desire to be with you again.

The Obsession Formula

When you're desperate to win her back, you need to become more than just a passing thought – you need to be her ultimate obsession. The Obsession Formula is designed to make her fantasize about reuniting with you and see you as her perfect match. Here's how to embed yourself deep in her subconscious and become her ultimate desire.

Making her fantasize about reuniting with you

- **The "Dream Sequence Implant":**
  - Casually mention having a vivid dream about her to a mutual friend
  - Ensure the friend tells her, but don't provide details about the dream
  - She'll start dreaming about you too, creating a subconscious connection

21 PSYCHOLOGICAL TRIGGERS TO MAKE YOUR EX BEG YOU FOR A SECOND CHANCE

PART 5: REIGNITING HER EMOTIONAL HOT BUTTONS

- **The "Future Self Projection":**
    - Start embodying the man she always wanted you to become
    - Subtly showcase these changes through social media or mutual friends
    - She'll start imagining a future with this new, improved version of you
- **The "Tantric Text Technique":**
    - Send her a text that starts to describe a passionate moment you shared
    - Cut the message off abruptly, as if sent by mistake
    - Her mind will race, completing the scene and reliving the passion
- **The "Sensory Memory Trigger":**
    - Leave a small item that reminds her of an intimate moment (e.g., a ticket stub from a concert)
    - Place it where she'll find it "accidentally"
    - The physical reminder will spark vivid memories and desires
- **The "Incomplete Fantasy" Method:**
    - Start telling a mutual friend about a romantic gesture you're planning
    - Make sure the friend mentions it to your ex, but without all the details
    - She'll fill in the blanks, imagining herself as the recipient of your affection

PART 5: REIGNITING HER EMOTIONAL HOT BUTTONS

- **Becoming her ultimate desire**
    - The "Primal Attraction Activation":
    - Engage in high-adrenaline activities (e.g., skydiving, rock climbing)
    - Ensure she sees or hears about these adventures
    - She'll subconsciously associate you with excitement and danger, heightening attraction
- **The "Forbidden Fruit" Technique:**
    - Cultivate an air of unavailability, hinting at other romantic prospects
    - Let her overhear conversations about your dating life, but keep details vague
    - She'll start seeing you as a prize to be won back
- **The "Emotional Rollercoaster" Strategy:**
    - Alternate between warm, engaging behavior and cool distance
    - This unpredictability will keep her emotionally invested and craving your attention
- **The "Alpha Male Showcase":**
    - Take on leadership roles in social or professional settings
    - Ensure stories of your confident, decisive actions reach her
    - She'll be reminded of your strength and capability, traits women find irresistible
- **The "Sexual Tension Amplifier":**
    - If you interact, use subtle touch and intense eye contact
    - Speak in a lower, slower voice, creating an intimate atmosphere
    - Leave her with a lingering sense of unfulfilled desire

PART 5: REIGNITING HER EMOTIONAL HOT BUTTONS

- **The "Prosperity Principle":**
    - Focus on rapidly advancing your career or business
    - Let news of your success spread through your social circle
    - She'll be drawn to your ambition and the lifestyle you can provide
- **The "Emotional Savior" Positioning:**
    - Become known as the person others turn to in times of need
    - Showcase your emotional intelligence and support for friends
    - She'll start seeing you as the stable, understanding partner she craves

By implementing these strategies, you're not just trying to win her back - you're becoming the man she can't resist. You're transforming into her ideal partner, the one she'll regret letting go.

Remember, this isn't about manipulation, but about genuine self-improvement and strategic presentation of your best self. As you become her obsession, she'll start to question why she ever left, and begin to fear losing you forever if she doesn't act soon.

This formula works by tapping into her deepest desires and fears. You're simultaneously becoming more attractive and seemingly less attainable, creating an irresistible pull that she won't be able to ignore.

PART 5: REIGNITING HER EMOTIONAL HOT BUTTONS

In the next section, we'll explore how to use the "Future Projection" technique to paint an irresistible picture of your life together that she can't help but want to be part of.

PART 6:

Becoming Her Ultimate Desire

21 Psychological Triggers to Make Her
Beg You for a Second Chance

PART 6: BECOMING HER ULTIMATE DESIRE

Future Projection

When you're desperate to win her back, you need to make her see a future with you that's so compelling, she can't bear to miss out on it. Future Projection is about painting a vivid, irresistible picture of your life together that will make her yearn to be part of your world again.

Painting an irresistible picture of your life together

- **The "Dream Life Blueprint":**
    - Create a detailed plan for an amazing future (career success, dream home, exotic travels)
    - Casually share parts of this plan with mutual friends, ensuring it gets back to her

PART 6: BECOMING HER ULTIMATE DESIRE

- o Make sure this future subtly includes elements she's always wanted
- **The "Parallel Universe" Tactic:**
  - o Start living the life you two once dreamed about together
  - o Share these experiences on social media or through mutual friends
  - o Let her see that the future she wanted is happening – without her
- **The "Nostalgic Future" Technique:**
  - o Revisit places you talked about going together, but with a twist
  - o For example, if you planned to visit Paris, go there for a business trip
  - o Share how the experience made you think of the plans you had together
- **The "Improved Partner Showcase":**
  - o Address the issues that caused problems in your relationship
  - o Demonstrate these changes in visible ways (e.g., if you were workaholic, show better work-life balance)
  - o Let her see that you've become the partner she always wanted you to be
- **The "Future Family Tease":**
  - o If you discussed having children, casually mention spending time with kids (nieces, nephews, friends' children)
  - o Share how much you enjoyed it and how it made you think about your own future family

PART 6: BECOMING HER ULTIMATE DESIRE

- Plant the seed in her mind of the amazing father you'd be

Making her yearn to be part of your future

- The "FOMO Accelerator":
    - Start planning exciting long-term projects or adventures
    - Ensure she hears about these plans through your social circle
    - Make these plans sound so amazing that she'll fear missing out if she's not with you
- The "Alternate Timeline" Method:
    - Live out the future you had planned together, but with a twist
    - For example, if you planned to start a business together, begin laying the groundwork solo
    - Let her see that her place in this exciting future is still open, but might not be for long
- The "Unfulfilled Dreams" Revival:
    - Revisit goals or dreams she had that weren't realized in your relationship
    - Start taking steps to support or achieve these dreams, even without her
    - Show her that you're still committed to the things that matter to her
- The "Power Couple" Visualization:
    - Start excelling in your career or personal projects
    - Subtly hint at how her skills would complement your success

PART 6: BECOMING HER ULTIMATE DESIRE

- Paint a picture of the unstoppable team you could be together
- **The "Emotional Security" Promise:**
  - Demonstrate emotional maturity and stability in all your interactions
  - Show how you've developed better communication and conflict resolution skills
  - Let her see that a future with you means emotional safety and understanding
- **The "Lifestyle Upgrade" Preview:**
  - Start enjoying the kind of lifestyle you know she's always wanted
  - Whether it's fitness, culture, travel, or luxury – live it and share it
  - Make her realize that this upgraded lifestyle could be hers if she's with you
- **The "Soulmate Reminder" Strategy:**
  - Engage in activities or hobbies that are uniquely "you" as a couple
  - Share these moments, reminding her of your special connection
  - Emphasize how rare and valuable your compatibility is

By masterfully implementing these Future Projection techniques, you're not just trying to win her back – you're making her realize that her best possible future is with you. You're showing her that all the dreams and plans you shared aren't just possible, they're happening right now.

PART 6: BECOMING HER ULTIMATE DESIRE

Remember, this isn't about creating a fantasy, but about genuinely building the life you both wanted and showing her that her place in it is still open. As she sees the amazing future unfolding – a future that aligns perfectly with her deepest desires – she'll be overcome with a yearning to be part of it.

This strategy works by tapping into her hopes, dreams, and fears. You're becoming the man she always knew you could be, living the life she always wanted, and showing her that she risks missing out on something extraordinary if she doesn't reconsider your relationship.

In the next section, we'll explore how to use Vulnerability and Authenticity to create a deep emotional connection that will make her feel like you're the only man who truly understands her.

Vulnerability and Authenticity
When you're desperate to win her back, you need to create a connection so profound that she feels you're the only man who truly understands her. Vulnerability and authenticity are your secret weapons to forge an unbreakable bond. Here's how to open up in a way that irresistibly draws her in and builds the deepest emotional intimacy she's ever experienced.

Opening up in a way that draws her in

PART 6: BECOMING HER ULTIMATE DESIRE

- **The "Emotional Striptease":**
  - Gradually reveal layers of your inner self, starting with lighter emotions and progressing to deeper vulnerabilities
  - Time these revelations carefully, creating a sense of privilege and intimacy
  - Make each disclosure feel like a special gift you're sharing only with her
- **The "Controlled Vulnerability" Technique:**
  - Share a personal struggle you're overcoming, but frame it as a journey of growth
  - Show both your vulnerability and your strength in addressing the issue
  - Let her see that you trust her enough to show your authentic self
- **The "Midnight Confession" Strategy:**
  - Choose a late-night moment to share a deep, personal truth
  - The timing taps into the natural intimacy of late-night conversations
  - She'll feel uniquely connected to you through this nocturnal honesty
- **The "Vulnerability Bait":**
  - Drop hints about a personal challenge or fear you're facing
  - When she inquires, initially hesitate to share, then open up
  - This creates a sense that she's earning your trust, deepening her investment

PART 6: BECOMING HER ULTIMATE DESIRE

- **The "Shared Secret" Bond:**
    - Confide in her about something you've never told anyone else
    - Emphasize that she's the only one you trust with this information
    - This exclusive knowledge creates a powerful, intimate connection

Building deep emotional intimacy

- **The "Emotional Echoing" Method:**
    - When she shares her feelings, reflect them back with your own similar experiences
    - Show that you not only understand but have felt the same way
    - This creates a sense of unparalleled emotional synchronicity
- **The "Deep Dive" Conversation:**
    - Initiate discussions about life's big questions (purpose, fears, dreams)
    - Share your genuine thoughts and encourage her to do the same
    - These profound exchanges create a unique intellectual and emotional bond
- **The "Vulnerability Challenge":**
    - Propose a mutual sharing of your biggest insecurities or past hurts
    - Go first, setting the tone for deep, authentic disclosure
    - This shared vulnerability creates an unbreakable trust between you

21 PSYCHOLOGICAL TRIGGERS TO MAKE YOUR EX BEG YOU FOR A SECOND CHANCE

PART 6: BECOMING HER ULTIMATE DESIRE

- **The "Emotional Time Capsule":**
  - Recall a moment when you felt intensely connected to her
  - Share the specific emotions and thoughts you had at that time
  - This reminds her of your unique emotional bond and reignites those feelings
- **The "Raw Truth" Revelation:**
  - Share an unfiltered truth about yourself, including flaws or mistakes
  - Follow it with how you're working to improve or what you've learned
  - This honest self-assessment shows maturity and self-awareness, traits she'll find irresistible
- **The "Empathy Amplifier":**
  - When she's facing a challenge, share a similar struggle you've overcome
  - Offer understanding without trying to fix her problem
  - Show that you can be her emotional support system, a shoulder she can always lean on
- **The "Soul-Baring Story":**
  - Share a deeply personal story that shaped who you are
  - Include details you've never told anyone, making her feel special
  - This level of openness creates an intense emotional intimacy she won't find elsewhere

PART 7: THE REUNION AND BEYOND

Remember, this meeting isn't about rehashing the past or pushing for immediate reconciliation. It's about creating a magnetic pull that will draw her back to you naturally. You're laying the foundation for a new, stronger relationship built on personal growth and deeper understanding.

This strategy works by balancing nostalgia with novelty, comfort with excitement. You're reminding her of why she fell for you initially while showcasing the improved version of yourself she's always dreamed of.

In the next section, we'll explore how to use "Rekindled Passion Techniques" to reignite the physical and emotional intimacy that will make her never want to leave again.

Rekindled Passion Techniques

Now that you've rekindled her interest, it's time to fan those sparks into a roaring flame of desire. These techniques will reignite the physical and emotional intimacy that made your relationship special, making her fall head over heels for you all over again.

Reigniting physical and emotional intimacy

- **The "Sensory Memory" Trigger:**
    - Recreate the scents, sounds, and tastes from your most passionate moments together

PART 7: THE REUNION AND BEYOND

- For example, wear the cologne you wore on your first date
- This taps into her subconscious, evoking powerful physical memories
- **The "Slow Burn" Escalation:**
  - Start with innocent touches (hand on arm, brief hug) and gradually increase intensity
  - Let each touch linger slightly longer than the last
  - This builds anticipation and sexual tension without being overtly sexual
- **The "Eye Contact Intensity" Method:**
  - Hold her gaze for 2-3 seconds longer than comfortable
  - Look at her lips briefly, then back to her eyes
  - This non-verbal communication signals desire and deepens your connection
- **The "Playful Physical Contact" Move:**
  - If you've been working out, casually mention your fitness routine
  - Then, with a playful smile, flex your arm and say, "Feel this — I think I might be turning into the Hulk!"
  - This creates a natural, light-hearted opportunity for her to touch you
  - Her physical contact with your improved physique will trigger attraction
- **The "Whisper Close" Technique:**
  - When speaking, move in close as if to whisper in her ear
  - Let your breath tickle her neck slightly
  - This intimate proximity will send shivers down her spine

PART 7: THE REUNION AND BEYOND

- **The "Passion Proxy" Strategy:**
  - Engage in activities that mimic the physiological responses of attraction (elevated heart rate, sweating)
  - Suggest dance classes, rock climbing, or other exciting physical activities
  - Her body will associate these sensations with you, rekindling attraction
  - Making her fall in love all over again
- **The "Emotional Time Machine":**
  - Recreate elements of your early dating phase
  - Surprise her with gestures reminiscent of when you first courted her
  - This taps into the powerful emotions from the start of your relationship
- **The "Vulnerability Vortex":**
  - Share a deep, personal fear or dream you've never told anyone
  - Follow up by saying, "I've never felt safe enough to share that with anyone else"
  - This level of openness creates an intense emotional bond
- **The "Future Fantasy" Projection:**
  - Paint a vivid picture of an amazing future together
  - Include specific details that align with her dreams and desires
  - Make this future feel tantalizingly close yet dependent on your reunion

PART 7: THE REUNION AND BEYOND

- **The "Appreciation Avalanche":**
    - Bombard her with genuine, specific compliments about her character
    - Focus on unique qualities that only someone who truly knows her would notice
    - This makes her feel deeply seen and valued
- **The "Passion Purpose" Alignment:**
    - Show how your personal growth aligns perfectly with her life goals
    - Demonstrate how you're now the ideal partner to support her dreams
    - This creates a sense that you're meant to be together
- **The "Emotional Echoing" Technique:**
    - When she expresses a feeling, reflect it back with heightened intensity
    - Show that you not only understand but feel things even more deeply than she does
    - This creates an unparalleled sense of emotional synchronicity
- **The "Intimacy Increaser" Challenge:**
    - Propose a series of increasingly intimate conversations or activities
    - Frame it as a fun challenge to rediscover each other
    - This gradually rebuilds your emotional and physical connection
- **The "Peak Emotion" Anchor:**
    - During a particularly positive moment, create a unique physical gesture

PART 7: THE REUNION AND BEYOND

- o Later, use this gesture to instantly recall those positive feelings
- o This creates a powerful emotional shortcut to positive associations with you
- **The "Unspoken Understanding" Bond:**
  - o Develop subtle, non-verbal cues that convey complex emotions
  - o Use these in public to create a sense of secret intimacy
  - o This reinforces your unique connection that no one else can replicate

By masterfully employing these Rekindled Passion Techniques, you're not just reminding her of your past love – you're creating a new, more powerful connection that surpasses anything she's ever experienced. You're becoming the man who understands her on a level so deep, it feels almost supernatural.

Remember, this isn't about recreating your old relationship. It's about forging a new, stronger bond that fulfills her deepest emotional and physical needs. As you implement these strategies, she'll find herself falling for you harder than ever before, unable to imagine her life without you in it.

This approach works by tapping into both her conscious and subconscious desires. You're stimulating her physically while also creating an emotional depth that she won't be able to find with anyone else.

PART 7: THE REUNION AND BEYOND

She'll realize that no other man can make her feel the way you do - physically excited, emotionally secure, and deeply understood.

In the final section, we'll explore the "Devotion Blueprint" - long-term strategies to keep her obsessed and prevent another breakup, ensuring she's yours forever.

The Devotion Blueprint
Now that you've won her back, it's crucial to ensure she stays madly in love with you. The Devotion Blueprint provides long-term strategies to keep her obsessed and prevent future breakups, securing a lasting commitment that grows stronger with time.

Long-term strategies to keep her obsessed

- **The "Intermittent Reinforcement" Technique:**
    - Alternate between periods of intense attention and slight unavailability
    - This creates a dopamine-driven cycle of anticipation and reward
    - She'll become addicted to the emotional highs you provide
- **The "Evolving Mystery" Approach:**
    - Continuously develop new skills, interests, and aspects of your personality
    - Reveal these gradually, always leaving more to discover
    - This keeps her constantly intrigued and eager to know more about you

PART 7: THE REUNION AND BEYOND

- **The "Relationship Milestone" Method:**
  - Create unique, personalized relationship milestones beyond typical anniversaries
  - Celebrate these moments with special rituals or surprises
  - This builds a rich tapestry of shared experiences only you two understand
- **The "Passion Project" Partnership:**
  - Initiate a long-term project or goal that requires both of your involvement
  - Choose something aligned with her interests but slightly out of her comfort zone
  - This creates a shared purpose and continuous growth together
- **The "Emotional Depth" Dive:**
  - Regularly engage in deep, meaningful conversations about life, dreams, and fears
  - Push the boundaries of emotional intimacy, always going a level deeper
  - This fulfills her need for profound connection that other men can't match
- **The "Unpredictable Romance" Strategy:**
  - Surprise her with romantic gestures at unexpected times
  - Vary the scale from grand gestures to small, thoughtful acts
  - This keeps the relationship exciting and prevents complacency

PART 7: THE REUNION AND BEYOND

- **The "Competitive Edge" Tactic:**
    - Subtly showcase your desirability to other women without crossing lines
    - Let her occasionally "catch" others admiring you
    - This triggers her competitive instincts, keeping her invested in winning your affection

Preventing future breakups and securing lasting commitment

- **The "Proactive Problem Solving" Approach:**
    - Regularly check in about potential issues before they become problems
    - Frame these discussions as "relationship optimization" rather than complaints
    - This shows maturity and commitment to continuous improvement
- **The "Individuality Encouragement" Method:**
    - Actively support her personal goals and interests, even those separate from you
    - Show genuine enthusiasm for her individual growth
    - This prevents feelings of lost identity that often lead to breakups
- **The "Shared Vision" Creation:**
    - Collaboratively craft a detailed vision of your future together
    - Regularly update and discuss this vision as your lives evolve
    - This aligns your long-term goals and reinforces your commitment

PART 7: THE REUNION AND BEYOND

- **The "Intimacy Balancing" Act:**
    - Maintain a careful balance of sexual passion and emotional closeness
    - Introduce new elements to your sex life while deepening emotional bonds
    - This satisfies both her physical and emotional needs, reducing temptation to look elsewhere
- **The "Appreciation Ritual" Institution:**
    - Establish daily or weekly rituals of expressing genuine appreciation
    - Focus on specific actions or qualities, not just general statements
    - This creates a positive feedback loop, encouraging more loving behavior
- **The "Growth Together" Commitment:**
    - Continuously seek ways to learn and grow as a couple
    - Attend workshops, read relationship books, or see a counselor proactively
    - This shows dedication to the relationship and prevents stagnation
- **The "Trust Reinforcement" System:**
    - Consistently follow through on promises, no matter how small
    - Be transparent about your activities and feelings
    - This builds unshakeable trust, the foundation of lasting commitment

PART 7: THE REUNION AND BEYOND

- **The "Conflict Transformation" Strategy:**
    - View disagreements as opportunities for deeper understanding
    - Develop a unique conflict resolution style that turns arguments into bonding experiences
    - This makes her feel safe expressing concerns, preventing resentment buildup
- **The "Relationship Reboot" Technique:**
    - Periodically "reset" your relationship with trips or new experiences
    - Use these moments to reaffirm your commitment and set new goals together
    - This prevents the relationship from feeling stale or taken for granted

By implementing this Devotion Blueprint, you're not just maintaining your relationship – you're continuously elevating it to new heights. You're creating a dynamic, evolving partnership that fulfills her deepest needs for excitement, security, and growth.

Remember, true lasting love isn't about grand gestures or perfect behavior. It's about consistent effort, genuine understanding, and a willingness to grow together. As you apply these strategies, you'll find that your relationship becomes stronger, more passionate, and more fulfilling with each passing day.

This blueprint works by addressing the core reasons relationships fail: boredom, lack of growth, unmet needs, and poor communication.

PART 7: THE REUNION AND BEYOND

By proactively tackling these issues, you're creating a relationship that not only endures but thrives over time.

Congratulations! You've now mastered the art of not just winning her back, but keeping her devoted to you for life. Your journey of love and growth together is just beginning, and with these tools at your disposal, you're set for a lifetime of passion, understanding, and deep connection.

Conclusion

Congratulations on making it to the end of this comprehensive guide. You've armed yourself with powerful strategies to win back the woman you love and create a relationship stronger than ever before. Let's recap the key strategies you've learned:

Recap of key strategies

- The No Contact Rule: Your foundation for success, allowing both emotional reset and personal growth.
- Understanding Her True Feelings: Decoding her actions and words to gauge her emotional state accurately
- The Scarcity Principle: Making yourself a rare and valuable commodity in her life.
- Social Media Mastery: Crafting an irresistible online presence that piques her curiosity and desire.
- The Jealousy Switch: Activating her competitive instincts without playing childish games.
- The Value Elevator: Dramatically increasing your perceived worth in her eyes.
- The Obsession Formula: Making her fantasize about reuniting with you.
- Future Projection: Painting an irresistible picture of your life together that she can't resist.

CONCLUSION

- The Perfect First Meeting: Melting her heart instantly when you finally reconnect.
- Rekindled Passion Techniques: Reigniting the physical and emotional intimacy that made your relationship special.
- The Devotion Blueprint: Ensuring she stays madly in love with you for the long haul.

Final words of encouragement

As you stand at the threshold of reclaiming your love, remember this: the journey you're about to embark on isn't just about getting her back. It's about becoming the best version of yourself – a man of confidence, value, and irresistible appeal.

The path ahead may seem daunting, but you now possess the tools and knowledge to succeed. Every strategy in this guide has been tested and proven effective by men just like you who refused to give up on true love.

Remember, your ex fell in love with you once before. With these new skills and your improved self, she'll fall for you even harder this time. You're not just rekindling an old flame; you're igniting a blaze that will burn brighter than ever before.

Stay committed to the process. There may be moments of doubt or setbacks, but keep pushing forward. Your dedication and transformation will not go unnoticed. Visualize your success.

CONCLUSION

See yourself holding her in your arms again, feeling her warmth, hearing her laughter. That future is within your grasp.

You have the power to turn your pain into triumph, your longing into fulfillment. The man she'll fall in love with again is already within you – now it's time to let him shine.
Go forward with confidence, determination, and an open heart. Your love story isn't over; the best chapters are yet to be written.

Remember, you're not just getting your ex back – you're creating a love so powerful, so unbreakable, that you'll never have to worry about losing her again.

Your journey to lasting love starts now. Embrace it, own it, and prepare for the passionate reunion that awaits you. Good luck, and may your love story become the envy of all who witness it.

Printed in Great Britain
by Amazon